SEAHORSES

For my favorite captain and crew:
Jim, Maddie, Max, and Pete
—J. K. C.

To the good people at Camp K-20
—C. W.

Thanks to Nicole Moy, who as a middle schooler studied and fell so in love with seahorses that she began making and selling custom jewelry and donating her profit to Project Seahorse, a small, international organization committed to conserving and sustaining use of the world's coastal marine ecosystems. Nicole generously shared her research and passion for seahorses with me for this book. In her honor, I will also donate royalties to Project Seahorse. For more information, please visit seahorse.fisheries.ubc.ca.

Henry Holt and Company, LLC, *Publishers since 1866*
175 Fifth Avenue, New York, New York 10010
mackids.com

Henry Holt® is a registered trademark of Henry Holt and Company, LLC.
Text copyright © 2012 by Jennifer Keats Curtis
Illustrations copyright © 2012 by Chad Wallace
All rights reserved.

Library of Congress Cataloging-in-Publication Data
Curtis, Jennifer Keats.
Seahorses / Jennifer Keats Curtis ; illustrated by Chad Wallace. — 1st ed.
p. cm.
Includes bibliographical references.
ISBN 978-0-8050-9239-4 (hc)
1. Seahorses—Juvenile literature. I. Wallace, Chad, ill. II. Title.
QL638.S9C87 2012   597'.6798—dc23   2011034059

First Edition—2012 / Designed by April Ward
The artwork in this book was created with digital media.
Printed in China by Toppan Leefung Printing Co. Ltd., Dongguan City, Guangdong Province

1 3 5 7 9 10 8 6 4 2

SEAHORSES

Jennifer Keats Curtis

Illustrated by Chad Wallace

Henry Holt and Company

New York

GLOSSARY:

Small fry: baby seahorse

Dorsal fin: fin on the seahorse's back

Pectoral fin: fin on each side of the seahorse's neck

Holdfast: surface seahorses can cling to so they don't float away

Krill: microscopic, shrimp-like animals

SOURCES INCLUDE:

Project Seahorse (seahorse.fisheries.ubc.ca)

Save Our Seahorses (sosmalaysia.org)

Maryland Sea Grant Extension (mdsg.umd.edu)

Monterey Bay Aquarium (montereybayaquarium.org)

AUTHOR'S NOTE

Seahorses look mythical, like dragons, but these magnificent, shy creatures are real.

Even though they don't look like it, seahorses are fish. They are found all over the world. Seahorses flutter through the ocean in places as far north as Norway and as far south as New Zealand.

This story is based on one of the more common species, the Mustang (*Hippocampus erectus*). Scientists believe there are more than thirty other species of seahorses. Males can give birth to anywhere from fifty to over a thousand babies at a time, but in the wild, very few live to become adults.

Once abundant, seahorses are, sadly, becoming rare. Their biggest threat? Humans. Development is destroying their habitat, leaving few sea grasses, corals, and other safe places to hide. And overfishing and the use of seahorses for medicine, crafts, and souvenirs have greatly reduced their population.

Since several species are considered threatened, some scientists have begun successfully breeding and raising seahorses (like the Mustang) in captivity as a way to reduce the number of seahorses taken out of the wild.

In the warm, salty water, a baby seahorse swirls and somersaults like a tiny gymnast performing on an invisible mat.

The baby seahorse's hard-plated,
spiny body tumbles alongside those of
his three hundred brothers and sisters.

No bigger than eyelashes, the babies—
called small fry—spin and whirl away
from one another like deflating balloons
in the ocean's gentle current.

Alone at last, the baby seahorse
uses the rapidly fluttering dorsal fin
on his back to push himself toward
a frond of green eelgrass.

Using the pectoral fins on each side of his neck to steer himself, he swims down until he can grasp the grass with his curly tail.

The little seahorse's body blushes like a
chameleon, changing from light brown to
green, until he is exactly the same color
as the grass he uses as his holdfast.

He perches peacefully in this secret
spot, perfectly camouflaged, eagerly
looking for food.

The newborn is ready to eat. Like a lizard, he can look in opposite directions at the same time. One eye stares left, the other turns to the right as he searches hungrily for krill, which look like small shrimp.

When he spies them, his horsey head quickly darts forward. He opens his long snout, puffs his cheeks, then slurps down ten tiny krill at once.

Click! Click! Click!

The small fry, like all seahorses, doesn't have a stomach, so he is always hungry. He could eat every two seconds and never feel full.

Over the next few months, the baby
seahorse grows rapidly, gulping the
little animals that float near him as he
hides in his small patch of the ocean's
grassy meadows.

With his wonderful ability to turn the same
color as his holdfast, the seahorse is completely
concealed from the crabs, big fish, and other
predators that would like to eat him.

Now the little seahorse is fully grown.

One morning, a female seahorse arrives.

She slowly swims toward him and fastens

her tail to the piece of grass next to

his. They sway, side by side, as their

courtship begins.

Although the female drifts off,
she returns early the next day to
greet her mate. This time, he floats
up to meet her. Dancing, they circle
each other, changing colors from
brown to green. His fins become very
dark brown as he waltzes around her
to music only they can hear.

The seahorse and his mate dance
the whole day away. They face each
other and float up through the water
toward the surface. Silently they
drift together for hours, their curly
tails tenderly entwined.

As night falls, the male seahorse's
pouch expands, filling with seawater.
His mate uses her special tube to
shift hundreds of eggs from her belly
into his waiting pouch. Within minutes,
her belly becomes flat. His pouch fills.

A few eggs float to the ocean
bottom, but almost all land safely
inside his pouch.

For nearly three weeks, the seahorse keeps
the eggs tucked safely inside his pouch as his
babies grow. While he is pregnant, he remains
quite still, eating only the krill that happen to
drift in front of him. His mate returns each
day, as if to keep him company.

One night, the eggs hatch. Like a bronco, the father seahorse bucks, then pumps his tail and pushes out the baby seahorses, each of which looks just like him. Hundreds of small fry burst into the water. As the father's belly deflates, his herd silently stampedes away, hungrily seeking food and holdfasts.

The last baby cartwheels past her father,

her tiny tail unraveling, then recoiling.

She rolls and turns away. Her new life

in the ocean has begun.